DOCUMENT EXERCISE WORKBOOK TO ACCOMPANY
VOLUME II: SINCE 1500

WORLD HISTORY

❖·❖

WILLIAM J. DUIKER
PENNSYLVANIA STATE UNIVERSITY

JACKSON J. SPIELVOGEL
PENNSYLVANIA STATE UNIVERSITY

PREPARED BY
DONNA VAN RAAPHORST
CUYAHOGA COMMUNITY COLLEGE

WEST PUBLISHING COMPANY
MINNEAPOLIS/ST. PAUL   NEW YORK   LOS ANGELES   SAN FRANCISCO

WEST'S COMMITMENT TO THE ENVIRONMENT

In 1906, West Publishing Company began recycling materials left over from the production of books. This began a tradition of efficient and responsible use of resources. Today, up to 95% of our legal books and 70% of our college texts and school texts are printed on recycled, acid-free stock. West also recycles nearly 22 million pounds of scrap paper annually—the equivalent of 181,717 trees. Since the 1960s, West has devised ways to capture and recycle waste inks, solvents, oils, and vapors created in the printing process. We also recycle plastics of all kinds, wood, glass, corrugated cardboard, and batteries, and have eliminated the use of Styrofoam book packaging. We at West are proud of the longevity and the scope of our commitment to the environment.

Production, Prepress, Printing and Binding by West Publishing Company.

ISBN 0–314–03797–7

For Barbara - my way station gift
until Alcatraz

Contents

Vol. II

Foreword

To The Student

To The Instructor

Foreword

The genesis of this work has been twenty some years of classroom instruction. Throughout this time period my students have been my best teachers and this book is a reflection of what has been most successful with them.

Many individuals helped to make these volumes possible. Nancy E. Crochiere, Clark Baxter, and especially Johanna Land at West Educational Publishing supported my ideas and efforts all along the way. No one could ask for a more supportive editor than Ms. Land, in particular, and I hope to work with her again on other projects for West.

Equally supportive were numerous individuals on the Western Campus of Cuyahoga Community College. Of special note are my Provost, Mr. Ronald M. Sobel, my departmental colleague, Ms. Mary Hovanec, my word processor, Ms. Marianne Lesniak, and Ms. Mikki Shackelton, a former student. Last but not least I am particularly grateful to my trusted and true friend Mary Kay Howard of John Carroll University for our numerous "brainstorming sessions." Without their assistance, aid, and cooperation this work would not have been possible.

To The Student

This supplement was written with you in mind. Specifically, it was designed to complement the textbook you are reading in your World History course, which is William Duiker and Jackson J. Spielvogel's <u>World History</u>, St. Paul, West Publishing Company. This small volume includes some documents that you will find in your text and several that are not.

The method of organization is chronological and the exercises that accompany the documents will progress from the relatively simple to the far more complex. The documents reflect the wide range of materials historians use in attempting to reconstruct the past. If you begin using this supplement when your coursework commences and continue to use it throughout the duration of your survey study of World History, you will develop a better understanding of historical source materials and of how historians study history.

To The Instructor

This slim volume was written to accompany William Duiker and Jackson J. Spielvogel's <u>World History</u>, St. Paul, West Publishing Company. Although some of the documents included here expand on the documents found in Duiker and Spielvogel, these exercises should be useful as a supplement to any text.

The materials within are arranged in a typical chronological fashion, but this book attempts to be more than simply another collection of documents. It endeavors to engage the student in a study of the past through a series of carefully constructed exercises using primary sources. These exercises are intended to develop thinking skills appropriate to the study of history. As such, they progress from those relatively simple in nature to those far more complex. More importantly, the exercises are ultimately aimed, as Russel H. Hvolbek has aptly written, for "the primary purpose of teaching history and the humanities (which) is to make students more aware of how their lives connect to the past human experience." This objective cannot be achieved by simply acquiring a body of knowledge. Students will come much closer to this goal if they learn how to seek out information and if they learn how to use this information. Hvolbek informs us that this is our ultimate responsibility in reevaluating how we teach our discipline with the provocative title of his essay--"History and Humanities: Teaching as Destructive of Certainty." (AHA <u>Perspectives</u>, January, 1991)

Chapter IX
Digging for Evidence

Make a list of sources you think some student a millenium from now would consult if he or she wished to discover the kinds of foods that were consumed in 20th century American society. Examine your list and see how many of those sources might have been available a millenium earlier. Not too many, right? Given you find this to be true, what source materials would you use to answer this important question about that period in time known generally as the Middle Ages? Below is a very brief list of possibilities:

1. Records from monasteries
2. Personal records and correspondence
3. Official records of knight's households
4. Guild records
5. Information about holiday and ceremonial feasts
6. Cooking manuals/cookbooks
7. Works of art
8. Poetry

Some of these possibilities should be of no surprise to you based on what you have already learned about this period in history. But what of the last three? Do you find it interesting to discover that cooking manuals or cookbooks existed? Did you assume they have always existed? One famous cooking manual, compiled by the master cooks of England's Richard II around 1390, was entitled The Forme of Cury. Here, for example, is a recipe for "salat": "Take parsel, sawge, garlec, chibollas . . . , oynons, leek, borage, myntes, porrectes . . . , fenel, and ton tressis . . . , rew, rosemarye, purslarye . . . ; lave, and woisshe hem clene; pike hem, pluk hem small with thyn . . . honde, and myng . . . hem ind raw oile. Lay on vynegar and salt, and serve it forth."(1)

A slightly older cookbook from France, a culture very often associated with excellent food, is that by Guillaume Tirel. Beginning as a mere scullion, he went on to work in the service of Philip VI of Valois and the Dauphin; was called to the kitchens of Charles V; and then, in 1375 wrote <u>Le Viandier</u>, the oldest French cookbook known to exist. Famous in its own day, it has remained so up to the present. In fact, <u>Le Viandier</u> is one of the first books to be put in print. Taillevent, as he liked to call himself, was much concerned with the secrets of making fine sauces, sops, and vegtables. Sops were an early form of pureed soups. They were made of wine flavored milk, saffron, and honey or other sweetners. Dead at the age of sixty-nine, Taillevent was buried beneath a tombstone picturing him in the dress of a sergeant at arms. Appropriately, his shield was embellished with three cooking pots.(2)

Early or late in their appearance, cookbooks are a most obvious source of information about dietary preferences. Did you ever think the final two on the list of possibilities could yield this type of information? Go to your own textbook and several others to look for illustrations of medieval art. What did you find? If little, dig further. Visit your college or university library and seek out art histories of the period. Note the things you find and put them aside for now.

Poetry! Probably you never ever considered this as a source. Yet one of the greatest masterpieces of world literature, Chaucer's <u>Canterbury Tales</u>, says much about food. Examine the excerpts provided. Answer the questions that follow as you interpret Chaucer.

DOCUMENT

> There also was a <u>Nun</u>, a Prioress,
>
> Her way of smiling very simple and coy.
>
> Her greatest oath was only 'By St Loy!'
>
> And she was known as Madam Eglantyne.

And well she sang a service, with a fine

Intoning through her nose, as was most seemly,

And she spoke daintily in French, extremely,

After the school of Stratford-atte-Bowe;

French in the Paris style she did not know.

At meat her manners were well taught withal;

No morsel from her lips did she let fall,

Nor dipped her fingers in the sauce too deep;

But she could carry a morsel up and keep

The smallest drop from falling on her breast.

For courtliness she had a special zest,

And she would wipe her upper lip so clean

That not a trace of grease was to be seen

Upon the cup when she had drunk; to eat,

She reached a hand sedately for the meat.

She certainly was very entertaining,

Pleasant and friendly in her ways, and straining

To counterfeit a courtly kind of grace,

A stately bearing fitting to her place,

And to seem dignified in all her dealings.

As for her sympathies and tender feelings,

She was so charitably solicitous

She used to weep if she but saw a mouse

Caught in a trap, if it were dead or bleeding.

And she had little dogs she would be feeding

With roasted flesh, or milk, or fine white bread.

And bitterly she wept if one were dead

Or someone took a stick and made it smart;

She was all sentiment and tender heart. . . .

.   .   .   .

A <u>Monk</u> there was, one of the finest sort

Who rode the country; hunting was his sport.

A manly man, to be an Abbot able;

Many a dainty horse he had in stable.

His bridle, when he rode, a man might hear

Jingling in a whistling wind as clear,

Aye, and as loud as does the chapel bell

Where my lord Monk was Prior of the cell.

The Rule of good St Benet or St Maur

As old and strict he tended to ignore;

He let go by the things of yesterday

And took the modern world's more spacious way.

He did not rate that text at a plucked hen

Which says that hunters are not holy men

And that a monk uncloistered is a mere

Fish out of water, flapping on the pier,

That is to say a monk out of his cloister.

That was a text he held not worth an oyster;

And I agreed and said his views were sound;

Was he to study till his head went round

Poring over books in cloisters? Must he toil

As Austin bade and till the very soil?

Was he to leave the world upon the shelf?

Let Austin have his labour to himself.

This Monk was therefore a good man to horse;

Greyhounds he had, as swift as birds, to course.

Hunting a hare or riding at a fence

Was all his fun, he spared for no expense.

I saw his sleeves were garnished at the hand

With fine grey fur, the finest in the land,

And on his hood, to fasten it at his chin

He had a wrought-gold cunningly fashioned pin;

Into a lover's knot it seemed to pass.

His head was bald and shone like looking-glass;

So did his face, as if it had been greased.

He was a fat and personable priest;

His prominent eyeballs never seemed to settle.

They glittered like the flames beneath a kettle;

Supple his boots, his horse in fine condition.

He was a prelate fit for exhibition,

He was not pale like a tormented soul.

He liked a fat swan best, and roasted whole.

His palfrey was as brown as is a berry.

.   .   .   .

There was a <u>Franklin</u> with him, it appeared;

White as a daisy-petal was his beard.

A sanguine man, high-coloured and benign,

He loved a morning sop of cake in wine.

He lived for pleasure and had always done,

For he was Epicurus' very son,

In whose opinion sensual delight

Was the one true felicity in sight.

As noted as St Julian was for bounty

He made his household free to all the County.

His bread, his ale were finest of the fine

And no one had a better stock of wine.

His house was never short of bake-meat pies,

Of fish and flesh, and these in such supplies

It positively snowed with meat and drink

And all the dainties that a man could think.

According to the seasons of the year

Changes of dish were ordered to appear.

He kept fat partridges in coops, beyond,

Many a bream and pike were in his pond.

Woe to the cook unless the sauce was hot

And sharp, or if he wasn't on the spot!

And in his hall a table stood arrayed

And ready all day long, with places laid. . . .(3)

QUESTIONS

1. What kinds of foods are mentioned in the <u>Tales</u>? Is there a considerable variety of food discussed in the poem? How many? List them.

2. Does it appear that food and drink are abundant? Does it seem that food and drink are important?

3. Find any descriptions of table manners. Describe them. Of what significance is this? How does it compare were someone to read this alongside Miss Manners or Emily Post?

4. Go back to the list of things you found when looking through your text and art books on the Middle Ages. How do these compare with what was in the <u>Canterbury Tales</u>? Write a brief essay on food and its importance in the Middle Ages.

5. If this topic is of particular interest to you, go further. Examine other works of poetry like <u>Carmina Burana</u>, and William Langland's <u>Piers the Ploughman</u>. Bon appetit!

Endnotes

1. William Harlan Hale and the editors of <u>Horizon Magazine</u>, <u>The Horizon Cookbook and Illustrated History of Eating and Drinking through the Ages</u> (Garden City, New York: American Heritage Publishing Co., Inc., 1968), 87.

2. <u>Ibid</u>., 85.

3. Geoffrey Chaucer, <u>The Canterbury Tales</u>, trans. Nevill Coghill (London: Penguin Books, 1951), 22-25; 28-29.

Chapter X
Philosophies of History

Surely you have heard the expression "History repeats itself." Just what exactly is the nature of such an expression? Is it merely another example of an historical generalization like those you learned to identify in Chapter VII? In a way yes it is, but it is more. It is more because it comes close to resembling a "law." A law because "it implies unvarying regularity" and therefore it might well be labeled a "predictive generalization."(1)

However true this might be, a predictive generalization is more and therefore better identified as a philosophy of history. "A philosophy of history is a systematizing of human knowledge and thought within the realm of historical fact." Furthermore, it is solely the personal judgment and interpretation of its originator and like believers who ascribe to it.(2)

Does this mean it is of no value to students of history like you? Quite to the contrary. Ponder the definition and the key word anew--systematizing; human knowledge and thought; and realm of historical fact. Is this not thought provoking? Does it not reaffirm the essential rationale for studying history as previously discussed? Could it not exert an influence on world events? Think of a philosophy of history that has exerted just such an influence.

At least three distinct philosophies of history can be identified. They include the cyclical (possibly fatalistic), the providential, and the progressive. By cyclical we really are saying that history repeats itself--history runs in cycles. In the Western world such a view prevailed from the time of the father of history, Herodotus, to the advent of Christianity. It could be argued it remains the paramount philosophy of history in many parts of the world today--

China, for example. The providential view of history emerged in the early Christian Era and maintained that the decisive event in history was the life of Christ "before which all mankind had been doomed, and after which all of the elect were saved."(3) The progressive philosophy of history fully developed around the early 18th century. Simply put, "mankind is getting better and better."(4)

Given these philosophies of history, how might you, the student, account for the rise and fall of great civilizations? Examine the two documents provided you that deal with the Muslim empires. Address yourself to the questions that come after them.

DOCUMENT 1

So saying, he [the Sultan] led them himself. And they, with a shout on the run and with a fearsome yell, went on ahead of the Sultan, pressing on up to the palisade. After a long and bitter struggle they hurled back the Romans [Byzantines] from there and climbed by force up the palisade. They dashed some of their foe down into the ditch between the great wall and the palisade, which was deep and hard to get out of, and they killed them there. The rest they drove back to the gate.

He had opened this gate in the great wall, so as to go easily over to the palisade. Now there was a great struggle there and great slaughter among those stationed there, for they were attacked by the heavy infantry and not a few others in irregular formation, who had been attracted from many points by the shouting. There the Emperor Constantine [Constantine XIII Palaeologus], with all who were with him, fell in gallant combat.

The heavy infantry were already streaming through the little gate into the City, and others had rushed in through the breach in the great wall. Then all the rest of the army, with a rush and a roar, poured in brilliantly and scattered all over the City. And the Sultan stood before the great wall, where the standard also was and the ensigns, and watched the proceedings. The day was already breaking. . . .

The soldiers fell on them [the citizens] with anger and great wrath. For one thing, they were actuated by the hardships of the siege. For another, some foolish people had hurled taunts and curses at them from the battlements all through the siege. Now, in general they killed so as to frighten all the City, and to terrorize and enslave all by the slaughter.

When they had had enough of murder, and the City was reduced to slavery, some of the troops turned to the mansions of the mighty, by bands and companies and divisions, for plunder and spoil. Others went to the robbing of churches, and others dispersed to the simple homes of the common people, stealing, robbing, plundering, killing, insulting, taking and enslaving men, women, and children, old and young, priests, monks--in short, every age and class. . . .

They say that many of the maidens, even at the mere unaccustomed sight and sound of these men, were terror-stricken and came near losing their very lives. And there were also honorable old men who were dragged by their white hair, and some of them beaten unmercifully. And well-born and beautiful young boys were carried off. . . .

After this the Sultan entered the City and looked about to see its great size, its situation, its grandeur and beauty, its teeming population, its loveliness, and the costliness of its churches and public buildings and of the private houses and community houses and those of the officials. . . . When he saw what a large number had been killed, and the ruin of the buildings, and the wholesale ruin and destruction of the City, he was filled with compassion and repented not a little at the destruction and plundering. Tears fell from his eyes as he groaned deeply and passionately: "What a city we have given over to plunder and destruction."

Thus he suffered in spirit. And indeed this was a great blow to us, in this one city, a disaster the like of which had occurred in no one of the great renowned cities of history, whether one speaks of the size of the captured City or of the bitterness and harshness of the deed. And no less did it astound all others than it did those who went through it and suffered, through the unreasonable and unusual character of the event and through the overwhelming and unheard-of horror of it.

As for the great City of Constantine, raised to a great height of glory and dominion and wealth in its own times, overshadowing to an infinite degree all the cities around it, renowned for its glory, wealth, authority, power, and greatness, and all its other qualities, it thus came to its end.(5)

DOCUMENT 2

They made one or two very poor charges on our right and left divisions. My troops making use of their bows, plied them with arrows, and drove them in upon their center. The troops on the right and the left of their center, being huddled together in one place, such confusion ensued, that the enemy, while totally unable to advance, found also no road by which they could flee. The sun had mounted spear-high when the onset of battle began, and the combat lasted till midday, when the enemy were completely broken and routed, and my friends victorious and exulting. By the grace and mercy of Almighty God, this arduous undertaking was rendered easy for me, and this mighty army, in the space of half a day, laid in the dust. Five or six thousand men were discovered lying slain, in one spot, near Ibrahim. We reckoned that the number lying slain, in different parts of this field of battle, amounted to fifteen or sixteen thousand men. On reaching Agra, we found, from the accounts of the natives of Hindustan, that forty or fifty thousand men had fallen in this field. After routing the enemy, we continued the pursuit, slaughtering, and making them prisoners. Those who were ahead, began to bring in the Amirs and Afghans as prisoners. They brought in a very great number of elephants with their drivers, and offered them to me as peshkesh. Having pursued the enemy to some distance, and supposing that Ibrahim had escaped from the battle, I appointed Kismai Mirza, Baba Chihreh, and

Bujkeh, with a party of my immediate adherents, to follow him in close pursuit down as far as Afra. Having passed through the middle of Ibrahim's camp, and visited his pavilions and accommodations, we encamped on the banks of the Siah-ab.

It was now afternoon prayers when Tahir Taberi, the younger brother of Khalifeh, having found Ibrahim lying dead amidst a number of slain, cut off his head, and brought it in. . . .

Yet, under such circumstances, and in spite of this power, placing my trust in God, and leaving behind me my old and inveterate enemy the Uzbeks, who had an army of a hundred thousand men, I advanced to meet so powerful a prince as Sultan Ibrahim, the lord of numerous armies, and emperor of extensive territories. In consideration of my confidence in Divine aid, the Most High God did not suffer the distress and hardships that I had undergone to be thrown away, but defeated my formidable enemy, and made me the conqueror of the noble country of Hindustan. This success I do not ascribe to my own strength, nor did this good fortune flow from my own efforts, but from the fountain of the favor and mercy of God. (6)

QUESTIONS

1. You are the philosopher of history and therefore free to make a personal judgment and interpretation. Ascribe a philosophy of history to each of the two documents in question. Explain your choice(s).

2.   Given what you have learned about Islam and the various Muslim civilizations, what philosophy of history do you think is most applicable to them? Why?

3.   Make an appointment with a philosophy or religion professor who is especially knowledgeable on this part of the world to find out if you answered the question above correctly. If you were not correct, reexamine the philosophies of history discussed in this chapter.

Endnotes

1. Lester D. Stephens, <u>Probing the Past: A Guide to the Study and Teaching of History</u> (Boston: Allyn and Bacon, Inc., 1974), 70.

2. Donald V. Gawronski, <u>History: Meaning and Method</u> (Iowa City: Sernoll, Inc., 1967), 19.

3. Allan Nevins, <u>The Gateway to History</u>, Rev. ed. (Boston: D. C. Heath and Company, 1938; Garden City, New York: Doubleday & Company, Inc., Anchor Books, 1962), 265.

4. Gawronski, <u>History</u>, 22.

5. William H. McNeill and M. R. Waldham, <u>The Islamic World</u> (Chicago: The University of Chicago Press, 1973), 331-335.

6. <u>The Memoirs of Zehir-ed-Din Muhammed</u> Baber, trans. John Leyden and William Erskine (London: Longman and Cadell, 1826).

Chapter XI
Understanding Cultural
Transformation

Surely at this point in your course of study, a better realization
of the complexity of your task has become apparent. You are in
fact trying to come to some understanding of humanity and its historical variations throughout time and place. Indeed an ambitious
objective! One possible way to help achieve this objective is by
examining the ways in which different peoples and different cul-
tures reacted, interacted, and were transformed by each other. Be
sure you note the words <u>transformed by each other</u>, for all groups
do change, however imperceptibly it may seem, as a consequence of
their contact. Too often this is not understood even by very
sophisticated minds; especially when those minds have been trained
in one world, the Occidental for example. Thus attempts are made
to impose "Western-inspired schemes . . . to East Asia. . . ."
whether they fit very well or not.(1) It is to this very part of
the world, specifically Japan, that will serve as the focus of
concern in this chapter.

The 16th century ushered in an impressive series of momentous
changes in the Western world. For good reason this is called the
Renaissance (meaning rebirth) and encompasses the Reformation and
Age of Discovery. But what of other corners of the world? What of
Japan? Read or reread the appropriate chapter or sections of your
textbook to find out. Equally important, how did these two different civilizations respond to one another in perhaps the most
dramatic manifestation of the period--exploration and discovery?

Read carefully the document provided. Answer the questions that
follow as you attempt to come to terms with cultural transformation.

DOCUMENT

"There are two leaders among the traders, the one called Murashusa, and the other Christian Mota. In their hands they carried some-thing two or three feet long, straight on the outside with a passage inside, and made of a heavy substance. The inner passage runs through it although it is closed at the end. At its side there is an aperture which is the passageway for fire. Its shape defies comparison with anything I know. To use it, fill it with powder and small lead pellets. Set up a small . . . target on a bank. Grip the object in your hand, compose your body, and closing one eye, apply fire to the aperture. Then the pellet hits the target squarely. The explosion is like lightning and the report like thunder. Bystanders must cover their ears. . . . This thing with one blow can smash a mountain of silver and a wall of iron. If one sought to do mischief in another man's domain and he was touched by it, he would lose his life instantly. Needless to say this is also true for the deer and stag that ravage the plants in the fields."

Lord Tokitaka saw it and thought it was the wonder of wonders. He did not know its name at first nor the details of its use. Then someone called it "iron-arms," although it was not known whether the Chinese called it so, or whether it was so called only on our island. Thus, one day, Tokitaka spoke to the two alien leaders through an interpreter: "Incapable though I am, I should like to learn about it." Whereupon, the chiefs answered, also through an interpreter: "If you wish to learn about it, we shall teach you its mysteries." Tokitaka then asked, "What is its secret?" The chief replied: "The secret is to put your mind aright and close one eye." Tokitaka said: "The ancient sages have often taught how to set one's mind aright, and I have learned something of it. If the mind is not set aright, there will be no logic for what we say or do. Thus, I understand what you say about setting our minds aright. However, will it not impair our vision for objects at a distance if we close an eye? Why should we close an eye?" To which the chiefs replied: "That is because concentration is important in everything. When one concentrates, a broad vision is not necessary. To close an eye is not to dim one's eyesight but rather to project one's concentration farther. You should know this." Delighted, Tokitaka said: "That corresponds to what Lao Tzu has said, 'Good sight means seeing what is very small.'"

That year the festival day of the Ninth Month fell on the day of the Metal and the Boar. Thus, one fine morning the weapon was filled with powder and lead pellets, a target was set up more than a hundred paces away, and fire was applied to the weapon. At first the people were astonished; then they became frightened. But in the end they all said in unison: "We should like to learn!" Disregarding the high price of the arms, Tokitaka purchased from the aliens two pieces of the firearms for his family treasure. As for the art of grinding, sifting, and mixing of the powder,

Tokitaka let his retainer, Shinokawa Shoshiro, learn it. Tokitaka occupied himself, morning and night, and without rest in handling the arms. As a result, he was able to convert the misses of his early experiments into hits--a hundred hits in a hundred attempts . . . .(2)

QUESTIONS

1. How does Lord Tokitaka respond to his introduction to Western firearms? Is his response favorable, unfavorable, both? Be able to explain and defend your point of view.

2. Check the Endnotes or appropriate section of your textbook to determine who authored the document. Remembering what you learned in an early chapter of this book, Chapter VI, is your interpretation of Lord Tokitaka's response altered? How?

3. Reread the document carefully. Prepare yourself to debate both positions based on the following quote:

> In short, the major impact of the West on East Asian civilization seems to have been in modern technology and modern forms of organization. Western values such as the importance of the individual have had at best a secondary role. In the sense that modern means have been accepted more readily than traditional Western ends the great transformation of East Asia can be better discribed as "modernization" than as "Westernization."(3)

Endnotes

1. John K. Fairbank, Edwin O. Reischauer, and Albert M. Craig, <u>A History of East Asian Civilization, Vol. II: East Asia The Modern Transformation</u> (Boston: Houghton Mifflin Company, 1965), 4.

2. William De Bary, ed., <u>Sources of Japanese Tradition</u> (New York: Columbia University Press, 1958).

3. Fairbank, Reischauer, and Craig, <u>East Asia The Modern Transformation</u>, 7.

Chapter XII
Looking Twice at the Same Person

The long reign of Louis the XIV (1643-1715) brought to fruition the work of Cardinal Richelieu in his endeavors to strengthen royal power. It was in France, under the rule of the "Sun King," that there emerged a highly developed centralized state. Disorder and insecurity were gradually replaced by religious uniformity, state policy coordinated by mercantilism, and glorification of power. These were the hallmarks of 17th century European civilization and France had one of the most impressive practitioners in Louis.

With dictionary in hand, read through Louis XIV's conception of royal responsibility to his son. Absolutism and skills in reading autobiography are your concern in this important document. Answer each of the questions that follow the document.

DOCUMENT

Two things without doubt were absolutely necessary: very hard work

on my part, and a wise choice of persons capable of seconding it

. . . .

I laid a rule on myself to work regularly twice every day, and

for two or three hours each time with different persons, without

counting the hours which I passed privately and alone, nor the time which I was able to give on particular occasions to any special affairs that might arise. There was no moment when I did not permit people to talk to me about them provided they were urgent . . . .

I cannot tell you what fruit I gathered immediately I had taken this resolution. I felt myself, as it were, uplifted in thought and courage; I found myself quite another man, and with joy reproached myself for having been too long unaware of it. This first timidity, which a little self-judgment always produces and which at the beginning gave me pain, especially on occasions when I had to speak in public, disappeared in no time. The only thing I felt then was that I was King, and born to be one. I experience next a delicious feeling, hard to express, and which you will not know yourself except by tasting it as I have done.

For you must not imagine, my son, that the affairs of State are like some obscure and thorny path of learning, which may possibly have already wearied you, wherein the mind strives to raise itself with effort above its purview, repugnant to us as much as its difficulty. The function of Kings consists principally in allowing good sense to act, which always acts naturally and without effort. What we apply ourselves to is sometimes less difficult than what we do only for our amusement. Its usefulness always follows. A King, however skillful and enlightened be his ministers, cannot put his own hand to the work without its effects being seen. Success, which is agreeable in everything, even in the smallest matters, gratifies us in these as well as in the greatest, and there is no satisfaction to equal that of noting every day some progress in glorious and lofty enterprises, and in the happiness of the people which has been planned and thought out by oneself. All that is most necessary to this work is at the same time agreeable; for, in a word, my son, it is to have one's eyes open to the whole earth; to learn each hour the news concerning every province and every nation, the secrets of every court, the mood and the weaknesses of every Prince and of every foreign minister; to be well-informed on an infinite number of matters about which we are supposed to know nothing; to elicit from our subjects what they hide from us with the greatest care; to discover interests of those who come to us with quite contrary professions. I do not know of any other pleasure we would not renounce for that. . . .

QUESTIONS

1. What particulars does Louis XIV believe are important for his son to rule effectively? How are they representative of the 17th century hallmarks previously articulated?

2. Read through the document again and make a list of what you find admirable about Louis XIV.

3. Read the document for a third time and compile a list of these aspects of Louis you dislike.

4. Compare your two lists and write a two paragraph essay (a biographical vignette) on Louis. Is your vignette well-balanced? Is good biography a balanced presentation? Is real balance possible or does a biographer already have strong opinions about his or her subject? Think about your answer the next time you read a biography.

Endnotes

1. <u>A King's Lessons's in Statecraft: Louis XIV; Letters to His Heirs</u>, Vol. II trans. Herbert Wilson (London: Ernest Benn Limited, 1924), 48-50.

Chapter XIII
The Difficult Art of Biography

Biography is the medium through which the remaining secrets of the famous dead are taken from them and dumped out in full view of the world. The biographer at work, indeed, is like the professional burglar, breaking into a house, rifling through certain drawers that he has good reason to think contain jewelry and money, and triumphantly bearing his loot away. The voyeurism and busy bodyism that impel writers and readers of biography alike are obscured by an apparatus of scholarship designed to give the enterprise an appearance of banklike blandness and solidity. The biographer is portrayed almost as a benefactor. He is seen as sacrificing years of his life to his task, tirelessly sitting in archives and libraries and patiently conducting interviews with witnesses. There is no length he will not go to, and the more his book reflects his industry the more the reader believes that he is having an elevating literary experience rather than simply listening to backstairs gossip and reading other people's mail . . . .(1)

The above thought provoking quote informs you that the focus of this chapter will be biography. In a number of earlier exercises you dealt with issues that touched upon this most difficult genre. Do you remember what they were? It is important for you to do so as a student of history. Ponder this for a moment, for very often when you think of history (other than facts) you think of biography. Famous people are usually the focus and such people have great appeal to us. A number of your exercises in these volumes have centered around famous people for this and other obvious reasons.

Your task will be to learn how to read biography more carefully using the skills from a previous exercise. An ideal opportunity avails you when examining the Enlightenment and enlightened despotism. Of all the interesting enlightened despots--Frederick II of Prussia (1740-86), Joseph II of Austria (1780-90), Gustavus III of Sweden (1771-92)--Sophia Augusta Frederica, better known as Catherine the Great of Russia (1762-96), remains the most intriguing.

Do you remember what enlightened despotism is? Because it remains somewhat difficult to define, here is a review. It evolved out of divine right absolutism embodied best in the person of Louis XIV. But the enlightened despot said little about any divine claim to the throne. Authority was justified on the grounds of usefulness to the state or as Frederick the Great referred to himself, "first servant of the state." With this in mind they built roads, bridges, codified laws, established a professional bureaucracy, repressed localism and provincial autonomy. Owing no special responsibility to either God or church, they favored toleration in religious affairs. They were reformist and rational attempting to implement change through reason, which was to come quickly and was less subject to compromise. As two leading scholars of this period have written, "enlightened despotism . . . was an acceleration of the old institution of monarchy, which now put aside the quasi-sacred mantle in which it had clothed itself and undertook to justify itself in the cold light of reason and secular usefulness . . . ."(2)

Four excerpts follow. They are brief sketches of Catherine the Great. Because few of you will probably be history majors and even fewer professional historians, these vignettes come not from full-length biographies, but instead from assorted texts. Most likely these are the sources where you will encounter Catherine in your studies, so read them carefully as you answer the questions provided you after the documents. By the way, do you know what type of source material you are using?

DOCUMENT 1

Catherine was born as Sophie in 1729 to the ruling family of Anhalt-Zerbst, a small German state on the Baltic. Her education was undistinguished, and her financial and marital prospects were slender. Then in 1744 Empress Elizabeth invited her and her mother to the Russian court. . . . To stabilize Russia's political future, Elizabeth wanted Grand Duke Peter safely married. . . . At the Russian frontier, they were greeted as honored guests of the empress. Rumors spread that Sophie was destined to marry Peter, heir to the throne. Young Sophie, casting her spell over Elizabeth, resolved to remain in Russia. . . . Sophie paid court to Peter, who, by her own account, was ugly, immature, and boastful. She studied Russian assiduously, and won good will at the imperial court. Converted to Orthodoxy "without any effort," she was christened Catherine (Ekaterina Alekseevna) and in 1745 married Peter. Her seventeen-year cohabitation with that perpetual adolescent tested her patience and ambition fully. . . . Soon Paul was born, son of Catherine and probably the courtier Serge Saltykov. Catherine busied herself with amorous adventures, extensive reading, and the study of court politics. She came to the throne as the best-educated, most literate ruler in Russian history. Ambition, vitality, and political shrewdness were her outstanding traits. "I will rule or I shall die," she told the English ambassador in 1757. Frederick II wrote in 1778; "The empress of Russia is very proud, very ambitious, and very vain." Her actions as ruler confirmed the truth of his remarks.(3)

DOCUMENT 2

Shortly after Elizabeth brought Peter to Russia, she also selected for him a wife--Princess Sophia Frederica Augusta of Anhalt-Zerbst, who upon arriving in Russia in 1744, was given the name of Catherine. From inception the marriage was a classic example of incompatibility and infidelity. . . . Catherine . . . was German by birth, French in spirit, Russian and Orthodox by choice, and Machiavellian by training. She was charming, sensual, mature, clever, calculating, deceitful, and had a craving for love and power. . . .

Catherine II became Empress of Russia on July 9, 1762, not by any dynastic claims, nor by a popular revolution, nor by the grace of God, but by means of a successful military coup skillfully engineered by a handful of conspirators with the timely aid of palace guards. To maintain herself in power she condoned the murder of her husband and granted her zealous supporters land, money, and promotions. She forgave or punished lightly her innocent critics, but was brutal in her treatment of those who contemplated replacing her with Ivan VI, who, due to long imprisonment, had been reduced to insanity. . . .

Based on her actions and character she has been termed a dilettante, a hypocrite, an enigma, an enlightened despot, a brilliant adventuress, a reactionary, a glory-seeker, a successful politician, an ambitious opportunist, and a nymphomaniac. She has also been described as a ruler who harvested the seeds of her predecessors, a benevolent despot, a lawgiver, a journalist, a playwright, and an annotator of ancient chronicles. She excelled most, however, as a German who successfully promoted Russia's interests, and particularly, as the extraordinary mistress of twenty-one men.(4)

DOCUMENT 3

With the advent of Catherine II, we come to the most arresting personality to occupy the Russian throne since the death of Peter. Brought up in a petty German court, she found herself transplanted to St. Petersburg as a mere girl, living with a husband she detested, and forced to pick her way through the intrigues that flourished around the Empress Elizabeth. She managed to steer clear of trouble only by using her keen wits. Catherine fancied herself as an intellectual; she wrote plays, edited a satirical journal, and steeped herself in the literature of the Enlightenment. Both before and after ascending the throne she maintained a goodly supply of lovers, several of whom had important roles in affairs of state.(5)

DOCUMENT 4

Sophia Augusta Frederica, better known to history as Catherine the Great, was the daughter of a minor German prince, Christian Augustus of Anhalt-Zerbst. Married to the despicable Tsarevitch Peter III at the age of sixteen, and received into the Orthodox Church under the name of Catherine, this German princess passed several lonely years at the Russian court, where she had few friends and was shamelessly neglected by her husband. She consoled herself with wide reading, learned the Russian language, and identified herself so loyally with the interests of her adopted country . . . . Indiscriminate in her love affairs, and often Machiavellian in her politics, Catherine was none the less a woman of remarkable sagacity and proved an inspired leader. . . . (6)

QUESTIONS

1. Characterize these portrayals of Catherine the Great. Are they positive; negative; a little of both?

2. Draw some generalizations (remember what these are?) about Catherine based on the four provided sketches. Was she an enlightened despot? What is your evidence?

3. Compare these depictions of Catherine the Great with the other enlightened despots. How much is said about their character; their psychological make-up; their love life? How much do you think this has to do with Catherine's gender? Are powerful women investigated and studied by different standards then powerful men? If so, think about the possible reasons. Curious to test this out? Undertake this same exercise with Elizabeth I of England.

4. Go to your own textbook and see how Catherine has been charac-
    terized. How different is it from those sketches provided you
    in this exercise? Do the times have anything to do with this?
    Look up the publication dates for all five examples. Have
    societal changes occurred that might account for these differ-
    ences? What are they?

Endnotes

1. Janet Malcolm, "The Silent Woman - I," <u>The New Yorker</u>, 23 & 30 August 1993, 86.

2. R. R. Palmer and Joel Colton, <u>A History of the Modern World: To 1815</u>, 4th ed. (New York: Alfred A. Knopf, 1971), 336-37.

3. David MacKenzie and Michael W. Curran, <u>A History of Russia and the Soviet Union</u>, 3rd ed. (Chicago: The Dorsey Press, 1987), 318-319.

4. Basil Dmytryshyn, <u>A History of Russia</u> (Englewood Cliffs, New Jersey: Prentice-Hall, Inc., 1977), 281-84.

5. Crane Brinton, John B. Christopher, and Robert Lee Wolff, <u>A History of Civilization: 1715 to the Present, Vol. II</u>, 3rd ed. (Englewood Cliffs, New Jersey: Prentice-Hall, Inc., 1967), 65.

6. Wallace K. Ferguson and Geoffrey Bruun, <u>A Survey of European Civilization</u>, 3rd ed. (Boston: Houghton Mifflin Company, 1962), 542-43.

Chapter XIV
Developing the Skills of
Interdisciplinary History

Increasingly in the 1970's historians began to borrow the theories and methods of the social sciences.(1) So much has this become the case that, although you learned to think of history as a humanity in the first chapter of this book, others actually classify it as a social science. Such classifications may seem unimportant to you, but the theories and methods of the social sciences can enable the historian to better understand complex social phenomena. For example, how much richer is your understanding of a person like Louis XIV and Catherine the Great given a strong foundation in the principles of human behavior provided by the discipline of psychology?

Wouldn't this be true of sociology given you were to undertake an examination of social structure in Central and South America? In the two documents that are the focus of this chapter, you will engage in interdisciplinary history. This will help you appreciate the value of the social sciences in historical inquiry. These documents concern themselves with three essential concepts--race, class, and, caste. Read the definitions of these concepts and refer back to them as directed. Answer the questions that follow directly after them.

Race - "any people who are distinguished, or consider themselves distinguished, in social relations with other peoples, by their physical characteristics."(2)

Class - "According to Max Weber, a number of people who have a specific causal component of their life opportunities in common as a result of a common position in the labor market."(3)

Caste - "A stratified social system in which social position is entirely determined by parentage, with no provision for achieved status."(4)

DOCUMENT 1

One of the most deeply rooted evils of our country--an evil that merits the close attention of legislators when they frame our fundamental law--is the monstrous division of landed property.

While a few individuals possess immense areas of uncultivated land that could support millions of people, the great majority of Mexicans languish in a terrible poverty and are denied property, homes, and work. . . .

There are Mexican landowners who occupy (if one can give that name to a purely imaginary act) an extent of land greater than the areas of some of our sovereign states, greater even than that of one of several European states.

In this vast area, much of which lies idle, deserted, abandoned, awaiting the arms and labor of men, live four or five million Mexicans who know no other industry than agriculture, yet are without land or the means to work it, and who cannot emigrate in the hope of bettering their fortunes. They must either vegetate in idleness, turn to banditry, or accept the yoke of a landed monopolist who subjects them to intolerable conditions of life

. . . .

How can a hungry, naked, miserable people practice popular government? How can we proclaim the equal rights of men and leave the majority of the nation in conditions worse than those of helots or pariahs? How can we condemn slavery in words, while the lot of most of our fellow citizens is more grievous than that of the black slaves of Cuba or the United States? . . .

With some honorable exceptions, the rich landowners of Mexico, or the administrators who represent them, resemble the feudal lords of the Middle Ages. On his seignorial land, . . . the landowner makes and executes laws, administers justice and exercises civil power, imposes taxes and fines, has his own jails and irons, metes out punishments and tortures, monopolizes commerce, and forbids the conduct without his permission of any business but that of the estate. The judges or officials who exercise on the hacienda the powers attached to public authority are usually the master's servants or tenants, his retainers, incapable of enforcing any law but the will of the master.

An astounding variety of devices are employed to exploit the peons or tenants, to turn a profit from their sweat and labor. They are compelled to work without pay even on days traditionally set aside for rest. They must accept rotten seeds or sick animals whose cost is charged to their miserable wages. They must pay enormous parish fees that bear no relation to the scale of fees that the owner or majordomo has arranged beforehand with the parish priest. They must make all their purchases on the hacienda, using tokens or paper money that do not circulate elsewhere. At certain season of the year they are assigned articles of poor quality, whose price is set by the owner or majordomo, constituting a debt which they can never repay. They are forbidden to use pastures and woods, firewood and water, or even the wild fruit of the fields, save with the express permission of the master. In fine, they are subject to a completely unlimited and irresponsible power.(5)

DOCUMENT 2

The inhabitants may be divided into different castes or tribes, who derive their origin from a coalition of Whites, Negroes, and Indians. Of each of these we shall treat particularly.

The Whites may be divided into two classes, the Europeans and Creoles, or Whites born in the country. The former are commonly called Peninsulars, but are not numerous, most of them either return into Spain after acquiring a competent fortune, or remove up into inland provinces in order to increase it. Those who are settled at Cartagena, carry on the whole trade of that place, and live in opulence; whilst the other inhabitants are indigent, and reduced to have recourse to mean and hard labor for subsistence. The families of the White Creoles compose the landed interest; some of them have large estates, and are highly respected, because their ancestors came into the country invested with honorable posts, bringing their families with them when they settled here. . . .

Among the other tribes which are derived from an intermarriage of the Whites with the Negroes, the first are the Mulattoes. Next to these the <u>Tercerones</u>, produced from a White and a Mulatto . . . . After these follow the <u>Quarterones</u>, proceeding from a White and a <u>Terceron</u>. The last are the <u>Quinterones</u>, who owe their origin to a White and a <u>Quarteron</u>. This is the last gradation, there being no visible difference between them and the Whites, either in color or features. . . . Every person is so jealous of the order of their tribe or caste, that if, through inadvertence, you call them by a degree lower than what they actually are, they are highly offended. . . . These castes, from the Mulattoes, . . . are the mechanics of the city; the Whites, whether Creoles or Peninsulars, disdaining such a mean occupation follow nothing below merchandise. . . .

The inhabitants of Lima are composed of whites, or Spaniards, Negroes, Indians, Mestizos, and other castes, proceeding from the mixture of all three.

The Spanish families are very numerous. . . . Among these are reckoned a third or fourth part of the most distinguished nobility of Peru. . . . All these families live in a manner becoming their rank, having estates equal to their generous dispositions, keeping a great number of slaves and other domestics, and those who affect making the greatest figure, have coaches, while others content themselves with chaises, which are here so common, that no family of any substance is without one. . . . The funds to support these

expenses, which in other parts would ruin families, are their large
estates and plantations, civil and military employments or commerce, which is here accounted no derogation to families of the
greatest distinction; but by this commerce is not to be understood
the buying and selling by retail or in shops, every one trading
proportional to his character and substance. . . .

The Negroes, Mulattoes, and their descendants, form the
greater number of the inhabitants; and of these are the greatest
part of the mechanics. . . . The third, and last class of inhabitants are the Indians and Mestizos, but these are very small in
proportion to the largeness of the city, and the multitudes of the
second class. They are employed in agriculture, in making earthen
ware, and bringing all kinds of provisions to market, domestic
services being performed by Negroes and Mulattoes, either slaves or
free, though generally by the former.(6)

QUESTIONS

1. Read Document 1 as you have all of them up to this point--
   circling unfamiliar vocabulary, underlining main ideas, but
   without referring back to your definitions of race, class, and
   caste. Write out your interpretation of the document. What
   do you think of Mexican society? How much understanding do
   you have of the rich; of the poor?

2. Reread Document 1 in conjunction with the definitions of race,
   class, and caste. Write out your interpretation of the document. Compare what you wrote in your first interpretation and
   your second one. How are they different? How are they the
   same? In a paragraph or two, discuss how the sociological
   concepts of race, class, and caste enable you to better
   understand the social system of Mexico in 1856-57.

3. As you read Document 2, refer back to your definitions and identify where race, class, and caste are discussed. Be able to explain how these definitions enriched your understanding of the document.

4. Reexamine the documents and definitions and discuss how all three provide insights into the structure of the societies in question.

102

Endnotes

1. Michael Kammen, ed., <u>The Past Before Us: Contemporary Historical Writing in the United States</u> (Ithica, New York: Cornell University Press, 1980), 26.

2. Oliver C. Cox, <u>Caste, Class, and Race</u> (Garden City, New York: Doubleday, 1948), 402.

3. Robert R. Alford et al., <u>Society Today</u> (Del Mar, California: CRM Books, 1971), 572.

4. Paul B. Horton and Chester L. Hunt, <u>Sociology</u>, 2nd ed. (New York: McGraw Hill Book Company, 1968), 525.

5. Benjamin Keen, ed., <u>Latin American Civilization</u>, Vol. 2 (Boston: Houghton Mifflin, 1974), 270-272.

6. Keen, ed., <u>Latin American Civilization</u>, Vol. I, 223-224.

Chapter XV
The Influence of Ideas in History

During much of the 19th century and on into the early 20th century, the Western European nations came into direct contact with virtually all the inhabited areas of the world. In places like the great subcontinent of India, they intensified their endeavors. This outburst of activity, often labeled imperialism, had many complex causes. The more industrial nations--the United States, Great Britain, France, Germany, and eventually Japan--needed markets for their finished products and raw materials to supply their ever increasing machines and techniques of production. Once establishing these economic connections, they needed to be protected at all costs. In time, heretofore remote places in Africa, Asia, and Latin America became strategically important. But wealth and power were not the only reasons, for there were those who wished to transport Western values, traditions, and institutions abroad.

One of the more powerful underlying notions behind this European imperialism was an idea. An idea based on a conception of race which evolved into racism. "By racism is meant the doctrine that a man's behaviour is determined by stable inherited characters deriving from separate racial stocks having distinctive attributes and usually considered to stand to one another in relations of superiority and inferiority. . . ."(1)

What are the bases of ideas--fact, inference, opinion--behind the idea of racism? You must decide as you analyze the two documents that follow. The first is a well known piece by the British poet Rudyard Kipling. The second is the expressed thoughts of the governor-general of French Indochina, Albert Sarraut. Read each of them carefully and address the questions provided you.

DOCUMENT 1

Take up the White Man's burden--

Send forth the best ye breed--

Go bind your sons to exile

To serve your captives' needs;

To wait in heavy harness,

On fluttered folk and wild--

Your new-caught sullen peoples

Half-devil and half-child.

Take up the White Man's burden--

In patience to abide,

To veil the threat of terror

And check the show of pride;

By open speech and simple,

An hundred times made plain

To seek another's profit,

And work another's gain.

Take up the White Man's burden--

The savage wars of peace--

Fill full the mouth of Famine

And bid the sickness cease;

And when your goal is nearest

The end for others sought,

Watch sloth and heathen Folly

Bring all your hopes to nought.

Take up the White Man's burden--No tawdry rule of

   kings,

But toil of serf and sweeper--

The tale of common things.

The ports ye shall not enter,

The roads ye shall not tread,

Go mark them with your living,

And mark them with your dead.

Take up the White Man's burden--

And reap his old reward:

The blame of those ye better,

The hate of those ye guard--

The cry of hosts ye humour

(Ah, slowly!) toward the light:--

'Why brought he us from bondage,

Our loved Egyptian night?'

Take up the White Man's burden--

Ye dare not stoop to less--

Nor call too loud on Freedom

To cloke your weariness;

By all ye cry or whisper,

By all you leave or do,

The silent, sullen peoples

Shall weigh your gods and you.

Take up the White Man's burden--

Have done with childish days--

The lightly proferred laurel,

The easy, ungrudged praise.

Comes now, to search your manhood

Through all the thankless years,

Cold, edged with dear-bought wisdom,

The judgment of your peers!(2)

DOCUMENT 2

More important than any other rights is the right of all human
beings to have a better life on this planet through the more
effective utilization of material goods and moral wealth suscept-
ible to be distributed to all living persons. This process can
only take place through the solid collaboration of all races,
liberally exchanging their natural resources and the creative
faculties of their own genius. Nature has divided these faculties
and these resources unequally across the surface of the globe
through the unequal influence of climate, of fertility and

hereditary values. Its arbitrary devolution has localized, here and there, one from another, in the diversity, the dispersion and the contrast. Is it just, is it legitimate that such a state of things should be indefinitely prolonged? In the name of humanity, one can respond forcefully: No! A right which results in undermining the right of universal well-being is not a right. Humanity is universal throughout the globe. No race, no people has the right or the power to isolate itself egotistically from the movements and necessities of the universal life.(3)

QUESTIONS

1. Of Kipling's; of Sarraut's main ideas, which are fact; which are inference; which are opinion? Compile a list of each. Note: You are identifying type of statement so it does not matter what is correct or incorrect.

2. Take your list of each fact, inference, and opinion and explain the reason for your choice.

3. Explain the importance of identifying these basic classifications of statements.

4. Are the arguments of these two men a balance of all three classifications; two classifications; one classification? How should this influence the thinking of the historian using this information?

5. Using the definition of racism provided you in this chapter, determine if one or both of these men were racist. Imperialism as practiced earlier in history is no longer quite so powerful a force. Unfortunately the same cannot be said for racism.

Endnotes

1. Michael Banton, <u>Race Relations</u> (New York: Basic Books, Inc., Publishers, 1967), 8.

2. Rudyard Kipling, "The White Man's Burden," (New York: Bantam; Doubleday, Dell Publishing Group, Inc., 1920).

3. Quoted in Georges Garros, <u>Forceries Humaines</u> (Paris, 1926).

Chapter XVI
The Power of Numbers

With the advent of sophisticated technology and an ever increasing interdisciplinary thrust (economics, psychology, and sociology), historians have come to appreciate the importance of statistics. In many ways they have always used quantitative generalizations (Do you remember what generalizations are?) when using such words as "all," "many," "few," "a significant number," "less than significant," "a large percent," "the population of." Used this way, these words or expressions lack precision. Numbers, statistics, help historians achieve that greater degree of precision bearing in mind that ". . . no presentation is final, all measurements and descriptions are accurate only to a limited degree, all investigations are incomplete, and in formulation of the results there will always be a [shadow of uncertainty]."(1)

Statistics are helpful to historical study beyond giving a greater degree of accuracy. They allow investigation into areas difficult to probe with more conventional print materials. For example, one of the ways to determine the impact of the Industrial Revolution on societies is through the careful compilation and examination of statistics. Of course numbers do not speak for themselves and ultimately it is the historian who must draw from them meaning, implications, generalizations, and conclusions.

Like all source materials numbers must be dealt with carefully, but they present the researcher with some additional concerns. They might draw undue attention to one of the categories used to organized information--economics. Stop for a moment to recall the others. Numbers are also very powerful. They seem final. How often is a statistic thrown out to cinch an argument? Though numbers call for the investigation of new issues, as well as old ones, other equally important sources must still be consulted so as to present a balanced account of the past.

Examine the two documents provided--one a chart and the other a more conventional written source. Both are concerned with that period of history from the mid-18th century until around World War I, a period known as the Industrial Revolution. Like all great change, industrialization had both positive and negative consequences. Answer the questions that follow the documents and see if you can discover them.

DOCUMENT 1

Population of Selected Cities (In Thousands)

	17th C	1800	1850	1880	1900	1950 (city)	1950 (metro)
New York	5	64	696	1,912	3,437	7,900	13,300
London	150	959	2,681	4,767	6,581	8,325	10,200
Paris	200	600	1,422	2,799	3,670	4,950	6,350
Moscow	unknown	250	365	612	1,000	4,700	6,500
Berlin	20	172	500	1,321	2,712	3,345	3,900
Manchester	under 15	77	303	341	544	700	1,965
Vienna	100	247	444	1,104	1,675	1,615	1,900
Rome	130	153	175	300	463	1,625	1,625

R. R. Palmer, ed. Atlas of World History (Chicago: Rand McNally & Company, 1962), 194-95.

DOCUMENT 2

Testimony of the Commission of Medical Examiners

The account of the physical condition of the manufacturing population in the large towns in the North-eastern District of England is less favourable. It is of this district that the Commissioners state, "We have found undoubted instances of children five years old sent to work thirteen hours a day; and frequently children nine, ten, and eleven consigned to labour for fourteen and fifteen hours." The effects ascertained by the Commissioners in many cases are, "deformity," and in still more "stunted growth, relaxed muscles, and slender conformation:" "twisting of the ends of long bones, relaxation of the ligaments of the knees, ankles, and the like." "The representation that these effects are so common and universal as to enable some persons invariably to distinguish factory children from other children is, I have no hesitation in saying, an exaggerated and unfaithful picture of their general condition; at the same time it must be said, that the individual instances in which some one or other of those effects of severe labour are discernible are rather frequent than rare . . . . Upon the whole, there remains no doubt upon my mind, that under the system pursued in many of the factories, the children of the labouring classes stand in need of, and ought to have, legislative protection against the conspiracy insensibly formed between their masters and parents, to tax them to a degree of toil beyond their strength.

In conclusion, I think it has been clearly proved that children have been worked a most unreasonable and cruel length of time daily, and that even adults have been expected to do a certain quantity of labour which scarcely any human being is able to endure. I am of opinion no child under fourteen years of age should work in a factory of any description for more than eight hours a day. From fourteen upwards I would recommend that no individual should, under any circumstances, work more than twelve hours a day; although if practicable, as a physician, I would prefer the limitation of ten hours, for all persons who earn their bread by their industry."(2)

QUESTIONS

1. Study Document 1. What generalizations can you make? Consider population increases and where their occurrence was most striking. Recalling your knowledge of this period of history, are these variables related? Explain.

2. What possible implications can be drawn from population increases, the Industrial Revolution, living, and working conditions? Draw another generalization.

3. Read Document 2 and reexamine your answers to the previous questions. Do you have to alter them? How? Do so.

4. Write a one hundred and fifty word balanced account using both
    documents that addresses the following thesis statement:

        Despite its human toll, in the long run, the
        Industrial Revolution was worth the costs.

Endnotes

1. William O. Aydelotte, <u>Quantification in History</u> (Reading, Massachusetts: Addison-Wesley Publishing Company, 1971), 96.

2. Commission for Inquiry into the Employment of Children in Factories, <u>Second Report, with Minutes of Evidence and Reports by the Medical Commissioners</u>, Vol. V, Session 29 January - 20 August, 1833 (London: His Majesty's Printing Office, 1833), 5.

Chapter XVII
War Destroys Everything

The price of war is obvious and ironic, for of all the great
calamities that befall civilization--famine, drought, disease,
natural disasters--only war is truly preventable. Surely in your
reading on World War I it should have struck you that this great
tragedy did not have to occur!

Just consider the cost:

> The Allied and Associated powers are calculated to have
> mobilized more than 42,000,000 men . . . and to have lost
> more than 5,000,000 lives (Russia and France together
> contributing 3,000,000 dead). The Central Powers, with
> Turkey and Bulgaria, mobilized nearly 23,000,000 and lost
> nearly 3,400,000 lives (Germany and Austria-Hungary
> together contributing nearly 3,000,000). The direct war
> expenditure of the Allied and Associated powers is esti-
> mated, approximately at, U.S. $145,388,000,000 (including
> U.S., British, and French loans of $19,697,000,000 to
> other belligerents); that of the other side, at U.S.
> $63,018,000,008 (including German loans of
> $2,375,000,000).
>
> These figures take no account of the number of wounded
> combatants (more than 21,000,000 in all) or of the
> indirect cost of the war, which includes nearly
> $30,000,000,000 for property losses on land, $6,800,000
> for ships and cargo lost, $45,000,000 for loss of pro-
> duction, $1,750,000 for losses to the neutrals, and
> $1,000,000,000 for war relief.(1)

As if this were not enough the health of an American president was forever destroyed, the governments of Austria-Hungary, the Ottoman Empire, Germany, and Russia were to fall. In some cases this meant an end to dynasties that had ruled for three hundred years. The Romanovs not only fell from power in the midst of war and revolution, but met their maker at the hands of a Bolshevik firing squad. This included Nicholas II, his German-born wife Alexandra, and their children.

Symbolic of this weak-willed and inept ruler, Nicholas II could not even make his cousin, William II of Germany, understand his position and thus prevent the carnage that lay ahead. Both fell from power. William II outlived Nicholas II by twenty four years. He died a country gentleman at Doorn in the Netherlands on June 4, 1941. Only nineteen days remained before Hitler was to invade the Soviet Union in World War II.(2)

Read the last-minute telegrams--frequently referred to in history as the "Willy-Nicky" notes--between these two rulers and relatives. War destroys everything, even family relationships. You will be able to examine how as you answer the questions that follow the letters.

DOCUMENTS

Emperor William II to Tsar Nicholas II, July 28, 10:45 p.m.

I have heard with the greatest anxiety of the impression which is caused by the action of Austria-Hungary against Servia [Serbia]. The inscrupulous agitation which has been going on for years in Servia, has led to the revolting crime of which Archduke Franz Ferdinand has become a victim. The spirit which made the Servians murder their own King and his consort still dominates that country. Doubtless You will agree with me that both of us, You as well as I, and all other sovereigns, have a common interest to insist that all those who are responsible for this horrible murder shall suffer their deserved punishment . . . .

Your most sincere and devoted friend and cousin

(Signed) Wilhelm

Tsar Nicholas II to Emperor William II, July 29, 1:00 p.m.

I am glad that you are back in Germany. In this serious moment I ask you earnestly to help me. An ignominious war has been declared against a weak country and in Russia the indignation which I full share is tremendous. I fear that very soon I shall be unable to resist the pressure exercised upon me and that I shall be forced to take measures which will lead to war. To prevent a calamity as a European war would be, I urge You in the name of our old friendship to do all in Your power to restrain Your ally from going too far.

(Signed) Nicholas

Emperor William II to Tsar Nicholas II, July 29, 6:30 p.m.

I have received Your telegram and I share Your desire for the conservation of peace. However: I cannot - as I told You in my first telegram - consider the action of Austria-Hungary as an "ignominious war." Austria-Hungary knows from experience that the promises of Servia as long as they are merely on paper are entirely unreliable . . . . I believe that a direct understanding is possible and desirable between Your Government and Vienna, an understanding which I - as I have already telegraphed you - my Government endeavours to aid with all possible effort. Naturally military measures by Russia, which might be construed as a menace by Austria-Hungary, would accelerate a calamity which both of us desire to avoid and would undermine my position as mediator which - upon Your appeal to my friendship and aid - I willingly accepted.

(Signed) Wilhelm

Emperor William II to Tsar Nicholas II, July 30, 1:00 p.m.

My Ambassador has instructions to direct the attention of Your Government to the dangers and serious consequences of mobilisation. I have told You the same in my last telegram. Austria-Hungary has mobilised only against Servia, and only a part of her army. If Russia, as seems to be the case, according to Your advice and that of Your Government, mobilises against Austria-Hungary, the part of the mediator with which You have entrusted me in such friendly manner and which I have accepted upon Your express desire, is threatened if not made impossible. The entire weight of decision now rests upon Your shoulders, You have to bear the responsibility for a war or peace.

(Signed) Wilhelm

German Chancellor to German Ambassador at St. Petersburg, July 31,

URGENT

In spite of negotiations still pending and although we have up to this hour no preparations for mobilisation, Russia has mobilised her entire army and navy, hence also against us. On account of these Russian measures, we have been forced, for the safety of the country, to proclaim the threatening state of war, which does not yet imply mobilisation. Mobilisation, however, is bound to follow if Russia does not stop every measure of war against us and against Austria-Hungary within 12 hours, and notifies us definitely to this effect. Please do communicate this at once to M. Sasonof and wire hour of communication.(3)

QUESTIONS

1. What are the different positions articulated by these two men?

2. What are the concepts, principles they seem to share and want to preserve so as to prevent war and possibly save themselves?

3. Can you detect a deterioration in their relationship? What evidence can you cite?

4. Exactly how are these men related? What tragic consequences did it have--other than World War I? This will involve a little research in the library, but its an interesting, personally sad dimension to history.

Endnotes

1.   _Encyclopaedia Britannica_, 15th ed., s.v. "World Wars."

2.   _Encyclopaedia Britannica_, 15th ed., s.v. "William II, Emperor."

3.   W. E. Adams et al., eds., _The Western World: From 1700, Vol. II_ (New York: Dodd, Mead, and Co., 1968), 421-42.

Chapter XVIII
Morality and Historical Assessment

In the early morning of 6 August 1945, a
United States Army weather observation plane
took off from the Tinian air base toward the
Japanese interior. As the plane neared
Hiroshima City . . . it sent a message to the
B-29 Enola Gay, which was following it and
carrying the atomic bomb. . . . at 8:15 a.m.
the whole city was instantaneously covered by
a bluish-white glare. . . . the atomic bomb
[was] released at 8:15:17 a.m. at an altitude
of 9,600 meters: the atomic bomb exploded 43
seconds later. . . .

With the explosion of the atomic bomb, the
epicenter instantaneously reached a maximum
temperature of several million degrees
centigrade . . . with the formation of a
fireball, powerful heat rays and radiation
were emitted in all directions. . . .(1)

Thus ended, on this day, the lives of more than sixty thousand
Japanese, as four square miles of the city of Hiroshima were
incinerated in the explosion. Thus began the dawn of a new and
more horribly frightening age--the Nuclear Age. Three days later
another bomb, this time a plutonium one, fell on the city of
Nagasaki. Five days later the Japanese Cabinet agreed to surrender
and the war in the Pacific was at last over.

Then as well as now, the decision to use this weapon of unprece-
dented force is debated. The decision therefore brings to the
forefront two important factors confronting those who attempt to
study the past--making historical interpretations about controver-
sial decisions and making moral assessments about those decisions.
You will focus on the latter of these two in this chapter.

As you examine the document on Japan's major objective in World War
II--the creation of a so-called Great East Asia Co-prosperity
Sphere--keep in mind the following moral issue: "Is it right to
perform an inherently immoral act in order to achieve a good end
and avoid a massive evil?"(2)

DOCUMENT

Draft Plan for the Establishment of a Great East-Asia Co-prosperity
Sphere

The Plan. The Japanese empire is a manifestation of morality and

its special characteristic is the propagation of the Imperial Way.

It is necessary to foster the increased power of the empire, to

cause East Asia to return to its original form of independence and

co-prosperity by shaking off the yoke of Europe and America, and to

let its countries and peoples develop their respective abilities in

peaceful cooperation and secure livelihood.

The Form of East Asiatic Independence and Co-prosperity. The

states, their citizens, and resources, comprised in those areas

pertaining to the Pacific, Central Asia, and the Indian Oceans

formed into one general union are to be established as an autonomous zone of peaceful living and common prosperity on behalf of the peoples of the nations of East Asia. The area including Japan, Manchuria, North China, lower Yangtze River, and the Russian Maritime Province, forms the nucleus of the East Asiatic Union. The Japanese empire possesses a duty as the leader of the East Asiatic Union.

The above purpose presupposes the inevitable emancipation or independence of Eastern Siberia, China, Indo-China, the South Seas, Australia, and India.

Regional Division in the East Asiatic Union. In the Union of East Asia, the Japanese empire is at once the stabilizing power and the leading influence. To enable the empire actually to become the central influence in East Asia, the first necessity is the consolidation of the inner belt of East Asia; and the East Asiatic Sphere shall be divided as follows for this purpose:

The Inner Sphere--the vital sphere for the empire--includes Japan, Manchuria, North China, the lower Yangtze Area and the Russian Maritime area.

The Smaller Co-prosperity Sphere--the smaller self-supplying sphere of East Asia--includes the inner sphere plus Eastern Siberia, China, Indo-China and the South Seas.

The Greater Co-prosperity Sphere--the larger self-supplying sphere of East Asia--includes the smaller co-prosperity sphere, plus Australia, India, and island groups in the Pacific.

Outline of East Asiatic Administration. It is intended that the unification of Japan, Manchoukuo, and China in neighborly friendship be realized by the settlement of the Sino-Japanese problems through the crushing of hostile influences in the Chinese interior, and through the construction of a new China. . . . Aggressive American and British influences in East Asia shall be driven out of the area of Indo-China and the South Seas, and this area should be brought into our defense sphere. The war with Britain and America shall be prosecuted for that purpose. . . .

Chapter 3: Political Construction

Basic Plan. The realization of the great ideal of constructing Greater East Asia Co-prosperity requires not only the complete prosecution of the current Greater East Asia War but also pre-supposes another great war in the future. Therefore, the following two points must be made during the course of the next twenty years: (1) Preparation for war with the other spheres of the world; and (2) Unification and construction of the East Asia Smaller Co-prosperity Sphere.

The following are the basic principles for the political construction of East Asia, when the above two points are taken into consideration. . . .

The desires of the peoples in the sphere for their independence shall be respected and endeavors shall be made for their fulfillment, but proper and suitable forms of government shall be

decided for them in consideration of military and economic require-
ments and of the historical, political and cultural elements
peculiar to each area.

It must also be noted that the independence of various peoples
of East Asia should be based upon the idea of constructing East
Asia as "independent countries existing within the New Order of
East Asia" and that this conception differs from an independence
based on the idea of liberalism and national self-determination
. . . .

Occidental individualism and materialism shall be rejected and
a moral world view, the basic principle of whose morality shall be
the Imperial Way, shall be established. The ultimate object to be
achieved is not exploitation but co-prosperity and mutual help, not
competitive conflict but mutual assistance and mild peace, not a
formal view of equality but a view of order based on righteous
classification, not an idea of rights but an idea of service, and
not several world views but one unified world view.(3)

QUESTIONS

1. Based on your understanding of the Great East Asia Co-pros-
    perity Sphere, give an interpretation of Japanese intentions
    for Asia.

2. Provide a moral assessment of the Great East Asia Co-pros-
    perity Sphere. Compare and contrast your interpretation with
    your moral assessment. Be prepared to discuss the difference
    between interpretation and moral assessment.

3.   Even before the atomic bomb was ever dropped on Japan, scientists like Robert Oppenheimer had recognized the moral dilemma it posed for civilization. As he watched it tested from the control bunker in the New Mexico desert, he was reminded of part of the Hindu <u>Bhagavad-Gita</u>. "I am become death, destroyer of worlds."(4) On the other hand, James B. Conant, another architect of the bomb project, responded thusly to a critic after its use--"moral men had to commit immoral acts in a world at war. . . ."(5) Always with your document in mind, make a moral assessment of the decision to drop the bomb in a two hundred and fifty word essay.

Endnotes

1. The Committee for the Compilation of Materials on Damage Caused by the Atomic Bombs on Hiroshima and Nagasaki, <u>Hiroshima and Nagasaki: The Physical, Medical, and Social Effects of the Atomic Bombings</u> (New York: Basic Books, Inc., Publishers, 1981), 21-22.

2. Robert C. Batchelder, <u>The Irreversible Decision, 1939-1950</u> (Boston: Houghton Mifflin Company, 1962), 221.

3. William De Bary, ed., <u>Sources of Japanese Tradition</u> (New York: Columbia University Press, 1958).

4. Robert A. Divine et al., <u>America: Past and Present</u> (Glenville, Illinois: Scott, Foresman and Company, 1984), 801.

5. Daniel J. Kevles, review of <u>James B. Conant: Harvard to Hiroshima and the Making of the Nuclear Age</u>, by James G. Hershberg, <u>The New Yorker</u> 10 January 1994, 85.

Chapter XIX
Political Uses of the Past

The English Romantic poet Samuel Taylor Coleridge once wrote:

> If men could learn from history, what
> lessons it might teach us! But passion and
> party blind our eyes, and the light which
> experience gives is a lantern on the
> stern, which shines only on the waves
> behind us!(1)

Do you agree? Consider this quote and refresh your memory with the philosophies of history. You explored this issue in an earlier exercise and you must deal with it again as you examine the industrial miracle of modern Japan. How can you account for the fact that a country defeated and in ruins at the end of World War II is now the second greatest industrial nation in the world? Can you find the answer to this question by examining the history of the Japanese?

If your answer was yes, be very careful. Use of the past can be a valuable tool. Carried too far it can be equally dangerous. If this were not the case, why would so many governments try to control records of the past? If you have read George Orwell's 1984, you will remember that history was erased and altered on a regular basis. What would it be like to live in a country where you had no historical frame of reference? On the other hand, recall the experience of the United States in the tragedy of Vietnam. Wasn't this partially an example of policy makers and leaders imposing the past--the so-called lesson of Munich--in situations where it was not applicable? Wasn't it equally the failure of these same leaders and policy makers to understand the history and culture of the Vietnamese?

Reflect on these examples as you read and examine the following document. As always questions will be provided after it to help facilitate and deepen your understanding.

DOCUMENT

I realize that these are very trying times for Americans. Until very recently, the United States was the unrivaled military and economic leader of the free world. Now, suddenly, Japan seems to have usurped that economic power. Americans from all walks of life are upset, frustrated, and worried about their country.

Most of America's woes are self-made, but some prefer to blame Japan, saying that our market is closed to U.S.-made products and we are an unfair trader. Those who cannot take stock of themselves--whether an individual, company, or nation--face an uncertain future. I want to believe that the United States, with its enormous underlying strength, will pull itself together and come roaring back. Yet there are many worrisome signs.

In October 1989, <u>Newsweek</u> reported that most Americans viewed Japan as a greater threat than the Soviet Union. The word "threat" might be appropriate if Americans had attempted to put their house in order. Instead, Congress looks to Japan for a scapegoat, uses high-handed tactics, and tries to push us around. To confuse a hypothetical military foe with an economic competitor and stick a ridiculous label like "threat" on us shows how dangerously confused the United States is. It would be fairer and more productive if Americans stopped the arm-twisting and sanctions and got their country back into shape.

Japan can help by compromise and cooperation, but the outcome depends primarily on American efforts. Let's be candid. America's problem is not Japan's economic strength but its own industrial weakness. As many senior Japanese executives have pointed out, the fundamental cause is the endemic shortsightedness in U.S. board-rooms. Some uninformed Americans make long lists of the evils of Japanese-style management and demand corrective action. Of course, there are impediments to free trade in Japan, but our businessmen are always ready to make reasonable adjustments. Before pointing the finger at Tokyo and Osaka, Americans should deal first with the host of problems in their own backyard.

A Japanese friend of mine established his own company and built it into a medium-sized corporation with a U.S. subsidiary. He is convinced that the complete separation of capital and management in the United States hurts business.

In Japan, companies are either family owned and managed or there is a psychological solidarity between the shareholders and management. In the United States, professional managers run the company for the stockholders, who often become adversarial if dividends slide. What are the consequences of these different arrangements?

Managers who pursue immediate profits miss out on large midterm (ten-year) gains. But U.S. institutional investors do not care where a company will be a decade from now. They are only interested in getting a quick, high return on their capital. If earnings fall off a bit, the big boys unload the stock before its value drops.

I hope the United States is not too proud to roll up its sleeves and do whatever is necessary to revive its manufacturing industry and economy. Then, America's enormous potential in high-technology fields will bloom and contribute to the next era. U.S. attacks on Japan's trade practices and demands for reforms are not a black-and-white issue; some points are valid and others are not. One thing, however, is certain: American critics should take a cold shower and calm down.(2)

QUESTIONS

1. Is the author of the document, Shintaro Ishiwara, encouraging Americans to make use of the past, beware of misusing the past, or a combination of both? Make a three column list and cite specific examples of those you can identify.

2. What philosophy or philosophies of history are implied in the Coleridge quote? Explain your response.

3. Shintaro Ishiwara's message to the United States is quite clear. What is that message? Discuss specifically how that message relates to both the past and the future of these two great nations.

Endnotes

1. <u>The Oxford Dictionary of Quotations</u>, 3rd ed., "Coleridge, Samuel Taylor."

2. Shintaro Ishiwara, <u>The Japan That Can Say No</u> (New York: Simon & Schuster, 1989), 60-61.

Chapter XX
Everyone Their Own Historian

In the late 1980's people throughout the world watched in amazement as the Iron Curtain came down for its final call; as the Berlin Wall crashed into a pile of rubble; and, as the Soviet Union vanished as though a figment of their imaginations. The world would not go up in a giant mushroom cloud after all. A bright new peaceful future, based on a global vision, lay ahead, or did it?

This seems an appropriate question as these volumes are brought to a conclusion. Throughout them you have learned that history is much more than simply acquiring information and memorizing it for an assignment. You have learned that history is a process of inquiring; a process that requires certain inductive skills coupled with a keen intellect. You have learned basic techniques to better enable you to read, comprehend, and analyze historical source materials--primary, secondary, print, pictorial, and statistical. You have discovered some of the more philosophical dilemmas with which the historian must wrestle in his or her own work. Now it is your turn to apply as much of what you have learned as possible in this, your final exercise within.

In your textbook, World History, the former president of Czechoslovakia (he is now the president of the Czech State) is quoted from a speech delivered in 1990. These words by Vaclav Havel will be the only source material with which you will be provided. These words will also serve as the springboard for your investigation-- your topic of investigation.

Write a five page, double-spaced essay that does all of the following:

1. Focuses on at least one of the categories the historian uses to organize information (political, economic, religious, social, intellectual, scientific, technological, artistic).

2. Uses as many kinds of source material as possible. Note that you <u>must</u> include one oral interview and two newspapers. One local newspaper should be supplemented by a publication such as the New York <u>Times</u> or the Washington <u>Post</u>. These are available in your library.

3. Establishes clearly the perspective of Havel and indicates some understanding of his perspective. (The skills you learned about biography should be helpful.)

4. Takes careful note of the distinctions between fact, inference, and opinion.

5. Carefully deploys the historical skill of selection. This is especially crucial in gathering sources and information beyond Havel.

6. Makes some generalizations <u>or</u> draws some moral conclusions.

---

7. Any other skills, types of resource material, or philosophical issues you are able to appropriately and properly include will further enhance your grade.

Now read the Havel document. Agree or disagree with it based on what has happened in the world, your country, your state, or your local community.

DOCUMENT

For this reason, the salvation of this human world lies nowhere else than in the human heart, in the human power to reflect, in human meekness and in human responsibility.

Without a global revolution in the sphere of human consciousness, nothing will change for the better in the sphere of our being as humans, and the catastrophe toward which this world is headed - be it ecological, social, demographic or a general breakdown of civilization - will be unavoidable . . . .

In other words, we still don't know how to put morality ahead of politics, science and economics. We are still incapable of understanding that the only geniune backbone of all our actions, if they are to be moral, is responsibility.

Responsibility to something higher than my family, my country, my company, my success - responsibility to the order of being where all our actions are indelibly recorded and where and only where they will be properly judged.

The interpreter or mediator between us and this higher authority is what is traditionally referred to as human conscience! (1)

138

Endnotes

1.   Vaclav Havel, <u>The Washington Post</u>, 22 February 1990, Sect. A
      28 d.

DOCUMENTS

Chapter IX

From The Canterbury Tales, by Geoffrey Chaucer, translated by Nevill Coghill. Copyright (c) 1951 by Penguin Classics. Reprinted with permission of Penguin Books, Ltd.

Chapter X

From William H. McNeill and M. R. Waldham, The Islamic World, copyright (c) 1973 by The University of Chicago Press. Used with permission. From The Memoirs of Zehir-ed-Din Muhammed Baber, translated by John Leyden and William Erskine (London: Longman and Cadell, 1826).

Chapter XI

From Sources of Japanese Tradition by William De Bary, 1958, (c) Columbia University Press, New York. Reprinted with permission of the publisher.

Chapter XII

From A King's Lessons in Statecraft: Louis XIV: Letters to His Heirs, Vol. II, trans. by Herbert Wilson. Copyright (c) 1924 Ernest Benn Limited. Reprinted by permission of A & C Black Publishers Limited.

Chapter XIII

From A History of Russia and the Soviet Union, 3rd ed. by David MacKenzie and Michael W. Curren. Copyright (c) 1987 by The Dorsey Press. From A History of Russia by Basil Dmytryshyn. Copyright (c) 1977 Prentice-Hall, Inc. From A History of Civilization: 1715 to the Present, Vol. II, 3rd ed. by Crane Brinton, John B. Christopher, and Robert Lee Wolff. Copyright (c) 1967. Prentice-Hall, Inc. From A Survey of European Civilization, 3rd ed. by Wallace K. Ferguson and Geoffrey Brunn. Copyright (c) 1962. Houghton Mifflin Company. Permission given by the Estate of Geoffrey Brunn.

Chapter XIV

Excerpt from <u>Latin American Civilization</u> by Benjamin Keen, ed. (Boston: Houghton Mifflin, 1974) Vol. 2, pp. 270-272. Excerpt from <u>Latin American Civilization</u> by Benjamin Keen, ed. (Boston: Houghton Mifflin, 1974), Vol. I, pp. 223-224.

Chapter XV

<u>The White Man's Burden</u>
From <u>Verse</u> by Rudyard Kipling. Copyright (c) 1920 by Doubleday, a division of Bantam, Doubleday, Dell Publishing Group, Inc. Used with permission of the publisher.
Excerpt from <u>Forceries Humaines</u> by Georges Garros (Paris, 1926).

Chapter XVI

From <u>Atlas of World History</u> by R. R. Palmer. Copyright (c) 1962. Rand McNally & Company.
Testimony of the Commission of Medical Examiners. From Commission for Inquiry into the Employment of Children in Factories, <u>Second Report, with Minutes of Evidence and Reports by the Medical Commissioners</u>, Vol. V, Session 29 January - 20 August, 1833. His Majesty's Printing Office.

Chapter XVII

From <u>The Western World: From 1700, Vol. II</u>, ed. by W. E. Adams et al. Copyright (c) 1968. Dodd, Mead, and Co.

Chapter XVIII

From <u>Sources of Japanese Tradition</u> by William De Bary, 1958 (c) Columbia University Press, New York. Reprinted with permission of the publisher.

Chapter XIX

From <u>The Japan That Can Say No</u> by Shintaro Ishiwara (New York: Simon & Schuster, 1989), pp. 60-61.

Chapter XX

From <u>The Washington Post</u> by Vaclav Havel, 22 February 1990.